OVERLOOKED CREATIONS OF BLACK ART AND CULTURE

Who was the first African American TV star? Turn to page 14 to find out.

BY JAY LESLIE

Children's Press®
An imprint of Scholastic Inc.

Special thanks to our content consultant and sensitivity reader, Deirdre Lynn Hollman, Senior Curriculum Specialist from the Black Education Research Center at Teachers College, Columbia University.

Library of Congress Cataloging-in-Publication Data available
ISBN 978-1-5461-7814-9 (library binding) | ISBN 978-1-5461-7815-6 (paperback) | ISBN 978-1-5461-7816-3 (ebook)

10 9 8 7 6 5 4 3 2 1 26 27 28 29 30

Printed in China 62
First edition, 2026

Book design by Kathleen Petelinsek
Series produced by Spooky Cheetah Press

Photos ©: cover background and throughout: SlamBang/Dreamstime; cover main: Historic Collection/Alamy Images; 1: Photofest; 4 left: Imusic/Alamy Images; 4 top right: David Attie/Getty Images; 4 center right: Friedman-Abeles, NewYork/Wikimedia; 4 bottom right: TJ Roth/Sipa/AP Images; 5 top left: Comic Book Plus/Wikimedia; 5 top right: Norman Films/Wikimedia; 5 bottom: David Bailey, British Vogue © Condé Nast; 6 top: Thomas Eakins: Portrait of Henry O. Tanner/Wikimedia; 6 bottom left: Library of Congress; 7 top: Historic Collection/Alamy Images; 7 bottom: Strobridge & Co. Lith./Library of Congress; 8 top: The Miriam and Ira D. Wallach Division of Art, Prints and Photographs: Photography Collection, The New York Public Library; 8 bottom right: Gift of the White House Endowment Fund, 1995; 9 right: Purchase, funds graciously donated by Maclean's magazine, the Maxwell Cummings Family Foundation and Empire-Universal Films Ltd/Musee McCord; 9 left: Schomburg Center for Research in Black Culture, Photographs and Prints Division, The New York Public Library; 10 top: Rare Book and Special Collections Division/Library of Congress; 10 bottom: C. M. Battey/Library of Congress; 11 bottom right: Gina Rodgers/Alamy Images; 12 top: Harrison Studio/Wikimedia; 12 center: Heritage Art/Heritage Images/Getty Images; 12 bottom: Wikipedia; 13 top: Library of Congress; 13 center left: Harrison Studio/ Wikimedia; 13 center right: Library of Congress; 14 left: Photofest; 14 top right: William Morris Agency/Wikimedia; 14 center right: Records/Alamy Images; 15 top: Library of Congress; 15 bottom: Bettmann/Getty Images; 16 top: GAB Archive/Redferns/Getty Images; 16 bottom: 20th Century Fox/Photofest; 17 bottom left: 20th Century Fox Tv/Kobal/Shutterstock; 18 top, 18 bottom: Comic Book Plus/Wikimedia; 19 top: Division of Culture and the Arts, National Museum of American History, Smithsonian Institution; 19 center: Joe Bodego/Flickr; 19 bottom left: Billy Ireland Cartoon Library & Museum/The Ohio State University; 20 left: Radio Hall of Fame/Museum of Broadcast Communications; 20 top right: Hannans/Atlanta Journal-Constitution/AP Images; 21 left: Indiana University Archives of African American Music and Culture/Jack Gibson Collection, SC 14; 21 right: Indiana University Archives of African American Music and Culture/Jack Gibson Collection, SC 14_17; 22 top: Courtesy Atlanta University Center, Robert W. Woodruff Library Archives; 22 bottom left: Courtesy Madam C.J. Walker Museum; 23 top: Bettmann/Getty Images; 23 center: Lincoln University/Getty Images; 23 bottom: Everett/Shutterstock; 24 top left: Juan Cortez/Camera Press/Redux; 24 bottom right : David Bailey, British Vogue © Condé Nast; 25 top: Keystone Press/Alamy Images; 25 bottom: Patrice Habans/Paris Match via Getty Images; 26 top right: ANL/Shutterstock; 26 bottom left: Catmuuu/Wikimedia; 26 bottom right: Harry Morrison/WWD/Penske Media/Getty Images; 27 bottom left: Kevin Mazur/WireImage/Getty Images; 28 top left: Morton Broffman/Getty Images; 29 top: Anthony Barboza/ Getty Images; 29 left: Robert Abbott Sengstacke/Getty Images; 30 top: Ricky Flores/Getty Images; 30 bottom right: Granamour Weems Collection/Alamy Images; 31 top: Granamour Weems Collection/Alamy Images; 31 center right: Michael Ochs Archives/Getty Images; 31 bottom: Imusic/Alamy Images; 32 top: Norman Films/Wikimedia; 32 bottom: Denver Public Library/Bridgeman Images; 33 top: Courtesy North Fort Worth Historical Society/Wikimedia; 33 center left: Brian Branch Price/ZUMA Wire/Shutterstock; 34 top left: Historic Collection/Alamy Images; 34 top right: Rare Book and Special Collections Division/Library of Congress; 34 bottom left: Howard University Gallery of Art/Wikimedia; 34 bottom right: Scott Joplin/Wikimedia; 35 top left: Comic Book Plus/Wikimedia; 35 top center: David Bailey, British Vogue © Condé Nast; 35 top right: Granamour Weems Collection/Alamy Images; 35 bottom left: Friedman-Abeles, NewYork/Wikimedia; 35 bottom right: TJ Roth/Sipa/AP Images.

All other photos © Shutterstock.

TABLE OF CONTENTS

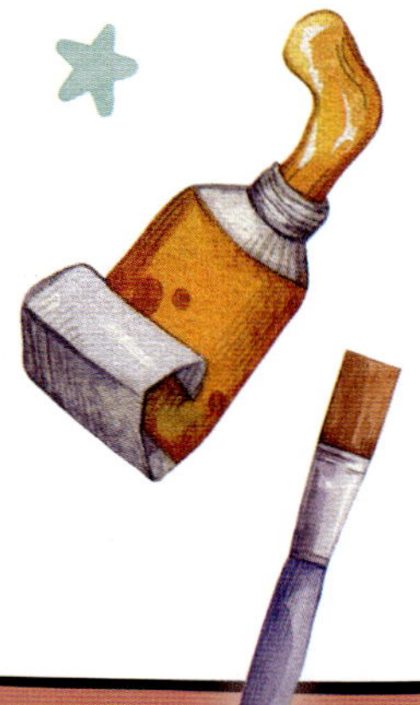

INTRODUCTION

When you think about powerful works of art and culture created by Black Americans, what comes to mind?

You might think of **Lorraine Hansberry's *A Raisin in the Sun*,** the groundbreaking play about the struggles of a Black family in America. Or maybe you've heard of the song **"What's Going On"** by Marvin Gaye. How about the ***Untitled*** painting by Jean-Michel Basquiat?

But there are probably many other important creations by Black people that might be unknown to you—lesser-known artistic and cultural works that have also shaped the history of the United States. This book shines a spotlight on ten of these "overlooked creations." They include revolutionary fine arts, groundbreaking books, **pioneering** shows, and more. Through all of them, Black Americans expressed their identities, spoke out against unfair treatment, inspired others, and made a real difference. Read on to discover how.

What was *All-Negro Comics*? Turn to page 18 to find out.

Who is this cowboy? Discover the answer on page 32.

Who was the first Black cover model? Turn to page 24 for the answer.

THE BANJO LESSON
A Powerful Portrait of Black Pride

In the 1800s, paintings often represented Black people in hurtful ways. Many paintings showed them as clowns. Some even compared them to animals. The paintings were meant to send unfavorable messages about Black people and how they compared to white people.

In 1893, **Henry Ossawa Tanner**, a young Black artist, created a painting that changed the way Black Americans were shown. The painting is called *The Banjo Lesson*. It portrays an elderly Black man teaching a little boy how to play the **banjo**.

Uncovered!

The banjo is a musical instrument that was created by **enslaved** Africans. It was a symbol of pride for Black communities. But white performers often used the banjo in **racist minstrel shows** that made fun of African Americans.

Tanner's painting shows a moment of love, wisdom, and pride. ***The Banjo Lesson*** is simple but powerful. Tanner represented Black people with the respect they deserved. The painting made many people think differently about how African Americans should be shown in art.

PRIMROSE & WEST'S BIG MINSTRELS
ALL WHITE PERFORMERS
THE GREAT NOVELTY PAIR
FREEZE BROTHERS THE WONDERFUL TAMBOURINE JUGGLERS
THE MOST MARVELOUS ACT ON THE AMERICAN STAGE
EACH SPINNING NO LESS THAN 16 TAMBOURINES
AT ONE TIME.

Hurtful Shows

Minstrel shows were popular in the 1800s and early 1900s. They were a racist type of entertainment. White actors painted their faces black and pretended to be Black people while acting silly, lazy, and foolish. Like some other works of art, these shows spread harmful **stereotypes**.

Who Was Henry Ossawa Tanner?

Henry Ossawa Tanner was born in 1859 in Pittsburgh, Pennsylvania. As a child, he became very interested in art. He dreamed of becoming a painter.

When Tanner was twenty years old, he began studying at the **Pennsylvania Academy of the Fine Arts**. That is the first and oldest art institution in the United States. Tanner was the only Black student in the entire school. Although he was incredibly skilled, he felt like he didn't fit in.

Uncovered!

Sand Dunes at Sunset, Atlantic City is another one of Tanner's paintings. In 1996, it became the first painting by a Black artist to be added to the White House's official permanent art collection.

For years, Tanner struggled to find success in the United States. Then, in 1891, he moved to Paris, France. Black artists were more accepted there. Tanner could paint and exhibit his work freely.

Tanner created *The Banjo Lesson* in 1893. The painting won many awards. It represented African Americans with dignity and pride.

Tanner became the first African American artist to achieve international fame. He paved the way for generations of artists to follow.

Moving Abroad

In the 1800s, African American artists had to fight for their place in the art world. Many went to Europe to find opportunities they were denied in the United States. Sculptor **Edmonia Lewis** moved to Italy. There, she created pieces that highlighted her African American and Native American roots. Painter **Robert Duncanson** found success in England. His landscapes were shown in London's best galleries.

THE BROWNIES' BOOK

A Magazine for Black Kids

In the early 1900s, it was hard for Black children to find books or magazines that showed people who looked like them. Most stories did not include Black characters. When they did, the characters were often shown in unfair or negative ways. **W.E.B. Du Bois** wanted Black kids to have a magazine that made them feel proud of who they were. So, in 1920, he helped create ***The Brownies' Book***. It was the first major magazine made especially for African American children.

The Thinker Who Took Action

W.E.B. Du Bois was a famous **activist** and scholar. He was the first African American person to earn a PhD from Harvard University. Du Bois also helped start the National Association for the Advancement of Colored People (NAACP). The NAACP is an organization that fights for equal rights for Black people. Du Bois's books and essays inspired civil rights activists for generations to come.

The Brownies' Book was filled with stories, poems, songs, and articles that celebrated African American culture. It included exciting **folktales**, inspiring stories about Black children, and articles about important figures in Black history. The magazine also featured photographs and letters from young readers across the country. For about **thirteen cents** a month, families could have the magazine delivered straight to their house. That is equal to $2.05 today.

Although *The Brownies' Book* lasted only about two years, it made a big difference. It showed Black children that their history and stories were important. It gave them a lot to be proud of. Even after the magazine's run came to an end, it inspired other publications to show Black children in a positive light.

Uncovered!

The Brownies' Book was the first magazine to publish a poem by **Langston Hughes**. He went on to become one of the most famous poets in America.

FIVE STAR SPORTS FINAL

A Home-Run Radio Show

In the 1930s, professional baseball was segregated. **Segregation** was the practice of separating Black and white people, and having different rules for each group. Black athletes were barred from playing in the whites-only Major Leagues. They had to play in the **Negro** Leagues, which received very little attention from the mainstream press. Then, in 1938, Sherman "Jocko" Maxwell changed the game with his radio show, *Five Star Sports Final*. Players in the Negro Leagues finally got the spotlight they deserved.

The Pittsburgh Crawfords played in the Negro Leagues.

N. Y. BLACK YANKEES

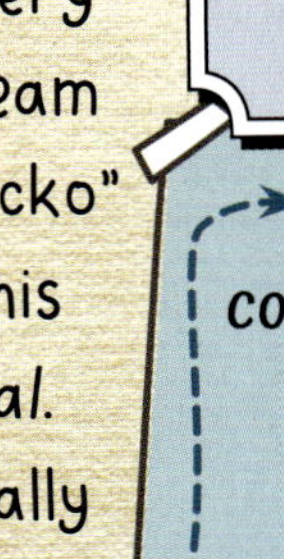

The term *Negro* was once commonly used to refer to Black people. It is now considered outdated and offensive. However, it remains acceptable when used in certain historical contexts, such as when referring to the Negro Leagues.

Who Was Sherman "Jocko" Maxwell?

Sherman "Jocko" Maxwell was born in Newark, New Jersey, in 1907. He loved baseball from an early age. In 1929, Maxwell became one of the first Black sports broadcasters in the United States. As the host of *Five Star Sports Final*, Maxwell focused most of his broadcasts on Negro Leagues teams.

Players to Know

The Negro Leagues were formed in 1920. For thirty years, Negro League games showcased legendary talents such as **Satchel Paige** and **Josh Gibson**. In 1947, **Jackie Robinson** became the first Black player to join modern Major League Baseball, ending segregation in the sport.

Maxwell's reporting preserved the stories of the Negro Leagues for future generations. It was crucial in keeping the **legacy** of Negro Leagues baseball alive. His dedication to promoting Black players made him a pioneer in sports journalism.

Maxwell was accepted into the Newark Athletic Hall of Fame in 1994.

Uncovered!
Sherman "Jocko" Maxwell covered more than one thousand baseball games.

THE ETHEL WATERS SHOW

The First Black Star on TV

On June 14, 1939, singer and actress **Ethel Waters** became the first African American performer to appear on television. And she did it by starring in her own show, *The Ethel Waters Show*.

The television special featured short **skits**, as well as a scene from Waters's Broadway play *Mamba's Daughters*. She performed alongside two other Black actresses, Georgette Harvey and Fredi Washington. Together, they showed the world that Black entertainers could shine on TV, too.

Waters was a popular jazz singer.

From Jim Crow to Jazz Clubs

Ethel Waters's journey to the top was not easy. She was born in Chester, Pennsylvania, in 1896, during the **Jim Crow** era. Waters's childhood was difficult. In addition to the hardships of segregation, Waters also had to overcome poverty. But her incredible voice helped her rise above her challenges.

Jim Crow is a term used to describe the racist laws and practices, such as segregation, that were the norm in the United States (especially in the South) from the 1870s to the 1960s.

Waters's voice was deep, soulful, and unique. Fans flocked to hear her sing jazz music in nightclubs and **vaudeville** theaters. Waters insisted on performing for **integrated** audiences. That meant that Black and white people could sit together. This was a brave move in an era when segregation was still the law of the United States.

Behind the Curtain: Vaudeville

Vaudeville was a popular form of live entertainment from the 1880s to the 1930s. Shows featured comedy, singing, dancing, and acrobatics. Most vaudeville theaters were segregated. But some theaters in the North allowed Black and white audience members to sit together.

From Music to Musicals

In 1933, Waters became the first Black actress to integrate Broadway when she performed in ***As Thousands Cheer***. Six years later, she made history when she debuted in *Mamba's Daughters*. It was the first time a Black actress had a leading part in a Broadway play.

Prime-Time Legacy

Eleven years after *The Ethel Waters Show*, Waters returned to television. This time, it was not just for one night. She had the starring role in *Beulah*. That was a sitcom about an African American housekeeper, or **"mammy."** Waters was one of the first Black actresses with a regular role on television.

A Harmful Myth

The mammy stereotype began after the **Civil War** as a way to pretend that enslaved women had been content, and even happy, to care for the families of their white enslavers. It ignored the inhumanity of **slavery** and tried to excuse the behavior of white Southerners before the war.

Hattie McDaniel was the first African American actor to win an Oscar. She won it for her role as Mammy in *Gone with the Wind*.

Waters later became the first Black woman nominated for a Primetime Emmy Award. That is an achievement award specifically for television. She showed the world that African Americans could be stars on both the stage and screen.

The Ethel Waters stamp was issued on September 1, 1994.

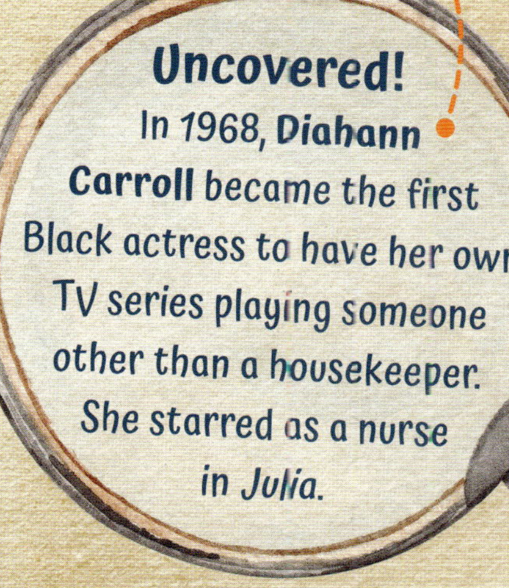

Uncovered!

In 1968, **Diahann Carroll** became the first Black actress to have her own TV series playing someone other than a housekeeper. She starred as a nurse in *Julia*.

ALL-NEGRO COMICS

A Comic Book That Saved the Day

As is often the case today, comic books in the 1940s were filled with superheroes, detectives, and action-packed adventures. But Black characters rarely appeared in the stories. And when they did, they were often shown in insulting, stereotypical ways. **Orrin C. Evans**, an African American journalist, changed the story when he cofounded *All-Negro Comics* and released its first issue in 1947. It was the first comic book written and illustrated entirely by African Americans.

All-Negro Comics featured exciting characters, including Lion Man, an African scientist who protected the jungle. There was also Ace Harlem, a detective solving crimes in his community. These characters were strong, smart, and heroic. They were exactly the kind of Black role models that were missing from comics.

Unfortunately, there was never a second issue of *All-Negro Comics*. Evans had the artwork ready, but he could not get the special paper he needed to print it. Paper companies refused to sell it to him.

Despite these obstacles, *All-Negro Comics* proved that Black creators could tell their own stories and create heroes who reflected a wider range of people. It opened the door for more **diverse** characters in comics, such as **Black Panther**, who appeared in 1966.

Wakanda Forever

Black Panther, created by Marvel Comics, was the first Black superhero in mainstream comics. Also known as T'Challa, Black Panther gave readers a powerful Black hero and strong, intelligent leader to admire. The character's success helped inspire more diversity in the comic book world.

Uncovered!

Jackie Ormes was the first Black American female cartoonist. Her 1937 newspaper **comic *Dixie to Harlem*** showed the difficulties of life as a Black woman traveling from the South to the North.

RADIO STATION WERD

Black Voices on Black Radio

In the 1940s, radio was still a major form of entertainment in America. Families gathered around their radios to listen to music, catch the news, and enjoy shows. But for African Americans, much of the programming did not feel like their own. For most of the '40s, no Black people owned radio stations. And only a few shows had Black presenters. Some stations played music for Black audiences. But they were run by white owners who did not fully understand the community.

That changed in 1949 when **Jesse Blayton, Sr.**, purchased **WERD**, a small radio station in Atlanta, Georgia. WERD became the first Black-owned and Black-operated radio station in the United States.

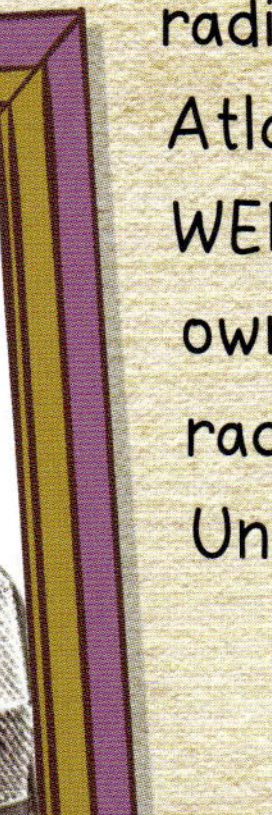

Uncovered!

Before WERD, *The All-Negro Hour* was the first radio program with only Black performers. It aired in Chicago in 1929. *The All-Negro Hour* featured skits and music.

Blayton understood that Black listeners needed more than catchy tunes. They needed a space where their stories were told, their issues were discussed, and their thoughts were heard. So he made sure that WERD delivered news, covered politics, and connected the community in a way no other station had. His vision grew WERD into more than just a radio station. It became a powerful voice for a community that had been left out of the conversation for too long.

JACK THE RAPPER
RADIO, RECORDS & RAP
TELLIN' IT LIKE IT "TIS" IS
A SUBSIDIARY OF
THE MOUSE HOUSE POST OFFICE BOX 2027, ORLANDO, FLORIDA 32802 (305)423-2328
© 1986 THE MOUSE HOUSE IN
AMERICA'S OLDEST, LARGEST CIRCULATED BLACK TRADE PUBLICATION
Volume Eleven • Issue 530 • June 11, 1986

WE SALUTE YOU BLACK MUSIC!

THE FAMILY OWES ALL OF YOU A DEBT OF GRATITUDE!

A Legend Is Born

Joseph Deighton Gibson, Jr., was one of the most popular voices on WERD. He was also known as "Jockey Jack" and later "**Jack the Rapper.**" Gibson was beloved for his fun, lively broadcasting style and for using Black slang on the radio. His energetic style helped shape "Black appeal" radio. That is a style of broadcasting that focuses on Black music and culture. This type of radio is still popular across the United States today.

Who Was Jesse Blayton, Sr.?

Jesse Blayton was born in Oklahoma in 1897. Despite the limitations of segregation, he worked his way up to become both a bank president and a **university professor** after moving to Atlanta. But Blayton's biggest achievement came when he purchased WERD in 1949.

When Blayton bought WERD, the first obstacle to overcome was its location. Black people were not allowed to use the restrooms in the building. Blayton moved WERD to Auburn Avenue, in the heart of Atlanta's Black community.

The former WERD studio is a museum today.

Uncovered!

Jesse Blayton was inducted into the Radio Hall of Fame in 1995. WERD continues to **broadcast online** today.

King of the Airwaves

WERD became a place where Black listeners could hear news about important issues like education and voting rights. **Dr. Martin Luther King, Jr.**, had an office in the same building as WERD. Whenever Dr. King wanted to make an announcement on the radio, he famously tapped on the ceiling with a broomstick to get the attention of the DJ upstairs.

How Black Radio Spread Civil Rights News

Across the United States, **Black radio stations** became a key part of the **Civil Rights Movement**. They shared news about rallies, speeches, and **protests** that mainstream stations ignored. Radio hosts invited civil rights leaders on air to discuss important issues. Many people learned about the NAACP, **voter registration drives**, and local politics through Black radio. That helped bring more people into the movement.

FIRST BLACK MODEL ON THE COVER OF BRITISH *VOGUE*

Redefining Beauty in the Fashion World

In the 1960s, beauty standards in the fashion world were dominated by the "European" look. Fair skin, light eyes, and straight hair were considered the definition of beauty. This was reflected in fashion magazines like *Vogue*. *Vogue* is one of the most influential fashion magazines in the world. Only white models were seen on the covers of these magazines.

Then, in 1966, **Donyale Luna** became the first Black model to appear on the cover of **British *Vogue***. In fact, she was the first Black model to appear on the cover of any major international fashion magazine.

Who Was Donyale Luna?

Donyale Luna was born Peggy Ann Freeman in Detroit, Michigan, in 1945. She moved to New York City when she was a teenager.

Luna's striking beauty caught the attention of top photographers, but she faced a tough challenge. Many magazines in the United States did not want to feature Black models. Those that did hire Black models often showed them as **"noble savages."**

As a child, Luna dreamed of becoming a movie star.

Luna at a photo shoot in 1966

When "Compliments" Become Insults

The noble savage stereotype at first might seem like a compliment. It presents people of color as pure and in harmony with nature. However, the stereotype is harmful because it suggests people of color are primitive. This stereotype also lumps together people from many different cultures. It ignores the fact that each culture has its own unique language, traditions, and history.

The First Black Supermodel

In December 1965, Luna moved to Europe and her career took off. Just three months later, in March 1966, she appeared on the cover of British *Vogue*. Soon after, *Harper's Bazaar* also chose Luna for its cover. That same year, American *Vogue* named her "Model of the Year." Luna was not just any model. She was the first Black supermodel.

Uncovered!
Luna worked closely with famous artists, such as painter **Salvador Dalí** and visual artist **Andy Warhol**.

Luna with Salvador Dalí

Luna sent a strong message: Beauty comes in many different forms. Today, models of all backgrounds can be seen on magazine covers, thanks in part to Donyale Luna.

Loving the Skin You're In

Winnie Harlow is a model who has vitiligo. That is a condition that causes parts of a person's skin to lose color. Like Donyale Luna, Harlow became famous by proudly embracing her unique look. Since the 2010s, Harlow has appeared in many fashion shows, magazines, and advertisements.

HOMECOMING
Poetry of the People

In the 1960s, the Civil Rights Movement was making progress toward racial equality. However, life for many Black Americans was still tough. Poverty, violence, and **discrimination** were everyday problems for many people. Sonia Sanchez, a poet originally from Alabama, wanted to tell the stories of the people in her community. In 1969, she released her first book of poetry, ***Homecoming***. It was bold, honest, and different from what people were used to reading.

Black Americans often struggled to gain basic rights and freedoms.

Uncovered!

As a child, Sanchez developed a stutter that made it difficult to talk. She began to spend more time with books instead of people. That led to her love of writing.

Who Is Sonia Sanchez?

Sonia Sanchez was born Wilsonia Benita Driver in 1934 in Birmingham, Alabama. She became a political activist who wrote powerful poems about the struggles and hopes of Black Americans. Sanchez's poems did not follow the usual poetry rules. Her writing style used the language and rhythms of everyday African American speech. That made her poems feel real and personal. Sanchez wrote about the pain and pride of Black communities, talking openly about racism and injustice. She also highlighted the strength and beauty of her people. This new way of writing caught the attention of many readers and made Sanchez a leader in the **Black Arts Movement**.

This mural, painted in 1967, celebrates African American heroes in many areas of Black art and culture.

Changing the Cultural Landscape

The Black Arts Movement began in the 1960s. That is when African American artists, writers, and musicians united to celebrate their identity. They created their own magazines, theaters, and publishing houses to promote Black stories and ideas. This movement also contributed to the establishment of African American studies programs at universities. Students could finally learn about Black history and culture in ways that had never been taught before.

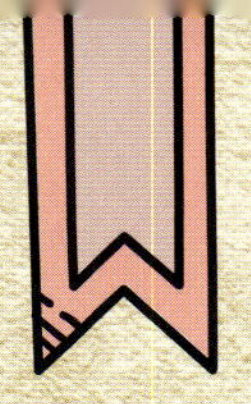

"RAPPER'S DELIGHT"
The Song That Introduced the World to Hip-Hop

Hip-hop is a musical genre that started in the streets of New York City, with DJs creating beats and rhymes at **block parties** in Black communities. Hip-hop was not played on the radio. And mainstream artists did not consider it "real" music. That changed in 1979 when the Sugarhill Gang released "Rapper's Delight."

Like hip-hop music, **breaking** started on the streets of New York City.

The Sugarhill Gang was made up of three rappers: **Wonder Mike**, **Big Bank Hank**, and **Master Gee**. The song they created was fun and full of energy. In it, the rappers told stories about their lives, their friends, and their love for music.

Uncovered!
The Sugarhill Gang recorded "Rapper's Delight" in a single take.

"Rapper's Delight" was the first rap song to be played on the radio. It sold more than **two million copies**. For the first time, a hip-hop song had broken into the mainstream. "Rapper's Delight" showed the world that hip-hop was more than just a passing trend—it was here to stay.

Sending a Message

After the success of "Rapper's Delight," more hip-hop songs began to break through. In 1982, Grandmaster Flash and the Furious Five dropped "The Message." The song stood out because it tackled serious issues like poverty and violence. "The Message" proved that hip-hop could be a powerful tool for talking about real-life struggles.

BILL PICKETT INVITATIONAL RODEO

A Rodeo to Remember

Black cowboys were an important part of the American West during the late nineteenth century. But they were often not allowed to participate in rodeos. Rodeos are competitions where people show off their skills in riding horses, roping cattle, and more. Then, in 1984, African American promoter Lu Vason founded the **Bill Pickett Invitational Rodeo**. It became the first African American touring rodeo in the world.

Black Cowboys Across the West

After the Civil War, many newly freed Black men became cowboys. Famous Black cowboys like Bill Pickett, Bass Reeves, and Nat Love helped shape the American West. About 25 percent of all cowboys were Black, yet they faced discrimination. For example, Black cowboys were often given the hardest jobs on cattle drives and ranches and were paid less than white cowboys.

The event is named after **Bill Pickett**, a Black cowboy who became a star in rodeos in the late 1800s and early 1900s. Pickett's skills made him a legend. He was accepted into the **ProRodeo Hall of Fame** in 1989, long after his death.

Lassoing the Legacy of Black Cowboys

At the Bill Pickett Invitational Rodeo, audiences can watch events like bull riding, calf roping, and **barrel racing**. But the rodeo is about more than just exciting competitions. It is a way to share the history of Black cowboys who helped shape the American West.

Uncovered!

Pickett invented an impressive **steer**-wrestling technique. He jumped from his horse, grabbed the steer by its horns, and pulled it to the ground. This daring move made him a rodeo star.

TIMELINE

You have learned about ten important artistic and cultural works that shaped our nation—ten overlooked creations of Black art and culture. Now you can connect them to some well-known works. And keep exploring. There are many more overlooked creations waiting to be celebrated!

1700s | 1800s | 1900s

1773
Phillis Wheatley's ***Poems on Various Subjects, Religious and Moral*** is published. It is the first book published by an African American poet.

1845
Narrative of the Life of Frederick Douglass, an American Slave is published. In it, Douglass tells the story of his life escaping slavery and fighting for freedom.

1867
Edmonia Lewis finishes her famous marble sculpture ***Forever Free***, which shows a man and woman celebrating their freedom after the end of slavery. Lewis was the first Black and Native American woman to gain international fame as an artist.

1893
Henry Ossawa Tanner paints ***The Banjo Lesson***.

1900
James Weldon Johnson writes **"Lift Every Voice and Sing."** Also known as the Black national anthem, the song celebrates hope and unity.

1902
Scott Joplin's **"The Entertainer"** becomes the biggest ragtime hit. Ragtime is fun, lively music with a special rhythm that skips beats.

1920
The Brownies' Book is published.

1938
The Five Star Sports Final begins broadcasting.

1939
The Ethel Waters Show airs.

The ten overlooked creations of Black art and culture featured in this book are on the top of the timeline. Well-known creations are on the bottom.

1947
All-Negro Comics publishes its first and only issue.

1949
Radio Station WERD becomes the first Black-owned radio station in the United States.

1966
Donyale Luna appears on the cover of British *Vogue*.

1969
Sonia Sanchez releases her first book of poetry, ***Homecoming***.

1979
"Rapper's Delight" is the first rap song played on the radio.

1984
The **Bill Pickett Invitational Rodeo** is started.

TODAY
Black artists continue to influence American arts and culture.

2000s

1959
Lorraine Hansberry's ***A Raisin in the Sun*** makes its Broadway debut. This play about a Black family trying to chase their dreams despite segregation was the first play on Broadway written by a Black woman.

1963
James Baldwin's ***The Fire Next Time*** is published. This powerful book calls for Black and white people to work together during the Civil Rights Movement.

1969
Maya Angelou releases her memoir ***I Know How the Caged Bird Sings***. It tells the poet's story of growing up as a Black girl facing racism in the early twentieth century.

1971
Marvin Gaye's ***What's Going On*** album is released. Among other things, the songs explore poverty, injustice, and the Vietnam War.

1982
Artist Jean-Michel Basquiat paints ***Untitled***. He uses bold images to show his Black identity and challenge racism, especially in the art world.

1987
August Wilson's ***Fences*** debuts on Broadway. The play, which is set in the 1950s, shows how racism holds people back from achieving their dreams.

GLOSSARY

activist (AK-tuh-vist) someone who supports a cause and believes in taking action to change things

breaking (BRAYK-ing) a style of energetic street dance featuring acrobatic moves and spins that developed along with hip-hop music

Civil Rights Movement (SIV-uhl RITES MOOV-muhnt) the fight for racial equality and citizenship in the United States that started in the mid-1950s and became famous for using nonviolent protests and civil disobedience to change unfair laws and practices

Civil War (SIV-uhl WOR) the war in the United States between the Confederacy, or Southern states, and the Union, or Northern states, that lasted from 1861 to 1865

discrimination (dis-krim-i-NAY-shuhn) prejudice or unfair behavior to others based on differences in such things as age, race, or gender

diverse (di-VURS) having many different types or kinds; varied

enslaved (en-SLAYVD) held involuntarily and forced to work without pay under threat of violence or death

folktales (FOHK-talez) stories that are passed down orally from one generation to the next

integrated (IN-tuh-gray-tid) changed to include people of all races

legacy (LEG-uh-see) something handed down from one generation to another

pioneering (pye-uh-NEER-ing) being one of the first to do something

protests (PROH-tests) demonstrations or statements against something

racist (RAY-sist) of or having to do with the belief that a particular race is better than others or that certain people can be treated unfairly or cruelly because of their race

segregation (seg-ri-GAY-shuhn) the practice of separating Black and white people, and having different rules for each group

skits (SKITS) short, usually funny plays

slavery (SLAY-vur-ee) the practice of holding people as property against their will, forcing them to work for no pay under threat of violence, and denying them the rights held by free persons

steer (STEER) a young male of the domestic cattle family, raised especially for its beef

stereotypes (STER-ee-oh-tipes) widely held but overly simplified ideas, opinions, or images of a person, group, or thing

INDEX

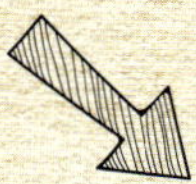

FURTHER READING

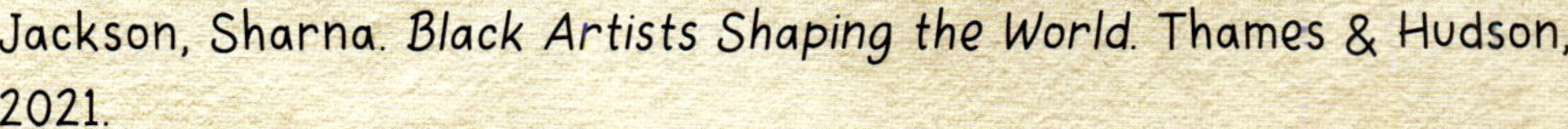

Jackson, Sharna. *Black Artists Shaping the World*. Thames & Hudson, 2021.

Leslie, Jay. *What I Must Tell the World: How Lorraine Hansberry Found Her Voice*. Zando, 2024.

Meadows, Michelle. *Jimmy's Rhythm & Blues: The Extraordinary Life of James Baldwin*. HarperCollins, 2024.

Reese, Cara. *Black Artists Rock! The Cool Kids' Guide A–Z*. Bea and Jo Press, 2022.

Weatherford, Carole Boston. *The Roots of Rap: 16 Bars on the 4 Pillars of Hip-Hop*. Little Bee Books, 2019.

Read the other books in this series:

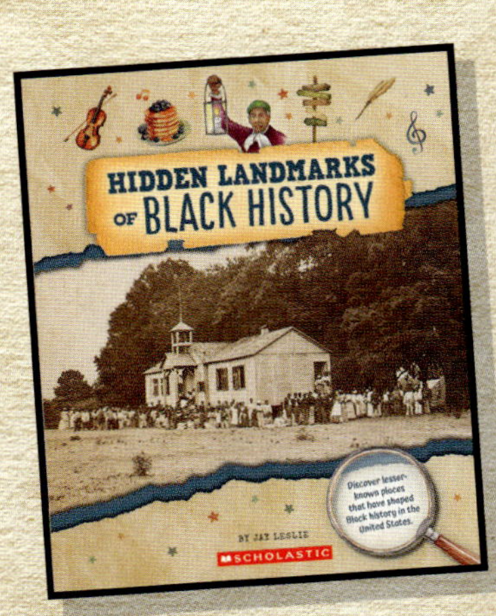

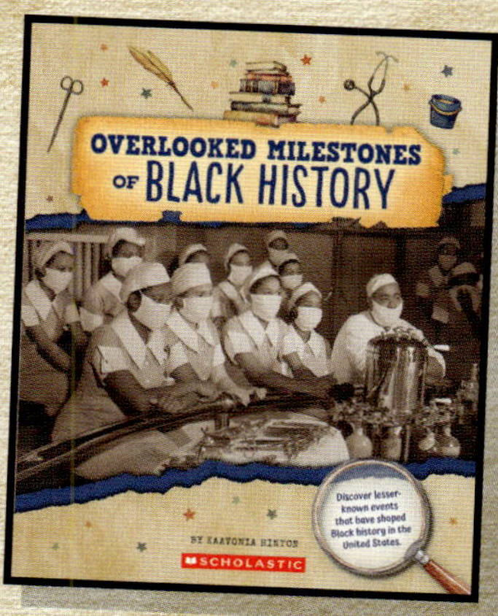

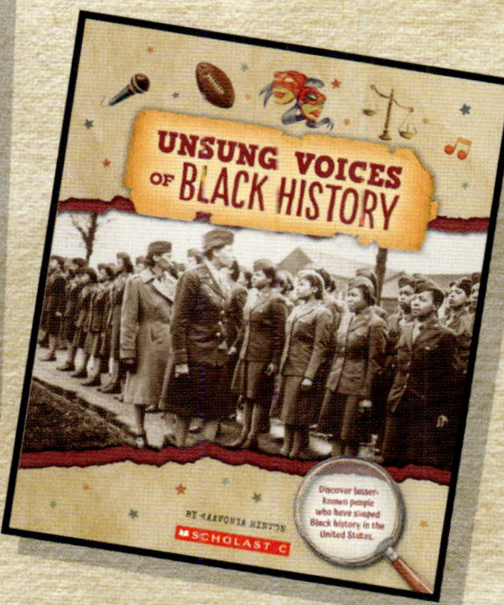

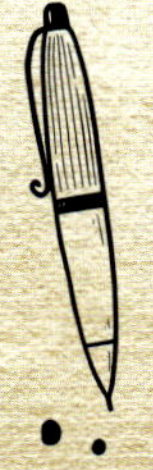

ABOUT THE AUTHOR

Jay Leslie has always loved to write. Everywhere she goes, she carries a notebook just in case she gets a new idea. Most of all, she loves to write the books that she wishes she'd had as a child.

Leslie grew up in the United States, but now she lives in Germany, where she spends her time writing novels, learning new languages, and backpacking through the Schwarzwald. Say hi at jay-leslie.com.